P9-CRZ-101

CCSS Genre Realistic Fiction

Essential Question
What makes you laugh?

by Emma Turner
illustrated by Elisabeth Eudes Pascal

CHAPTER 1

The Pranksters

Brad liked playing practical jokes, and he'd just had an idea for another good one. Brad's best friend Robbie liked pulling pranks, too, so Brad raced over to Robbie's house to tell him about it before school.

"I've got a great idea for a new joke," Brad said as he burst through Robbie's front door.

"Great minds think alike!" Robbie said. "I've got one, too!"

"You go first," said Brad.

"I'm on laundry duty this week," said Robbie. "All of the swim team towels are purple, right? Why don't we soak the towels in grape-flavored soda before we hang them up on the line? No one will notice because they won't look any different, but when the kids go to dry themselves, the purple soda will wipe off on their skin. They'll turn purple!"

"I'm not sure that's such a great idea—what if the purple won't wash off?" said Brad.

"Oh, I didn't think of that. You're probably right. What's your idea?" Robbie asked.

"I'm on lunchroom duty this week," said Brad. "I bought some super-real looking plastic flies from the joke shop in town. Let's put them on the lunch trays at school. That will really gross out some of the kids."

"That sounds great," said Robbie. "I can just imagine the looks on their faces!"

Half an hour before lunch, Brad reported for lunchroom duty as usual. He waited until the lunch lady had finished preparing the lasagna, and then he smiled sweetly at her and said, "I'll put the trays out today, Mrs. Jamieson."

Brad unzipped his backpack and took out the plastic flies he'd brought from home. He carefully sprinkled them under the rims of the plates, where they would be hidden from view at first glance.

Then he remembered the rubber worms in his pocket. He made a small hole in an apple and pushed one of the worms into the hole. Then he put the apple out on the counter with all the other fruit.

Soon, the lunchroom began to fill with kids. It wasn't long before there was a loud shriek. "Yuck! There are a bunch of dead flies on my lunch tray!" someone yelled.

"Eww!" one of the girls shouted. "There's a worm in my apple!"

Then the kids began to examine the "dead" flies more closely and soon realized that they weren't real.

The girl pulled the rubber worm out of the apple and held it up in the air. "Whose idea of a joke is this?" she asked, and she didn't look very amused at all.

CHAPTER 2

Time for More Pranks

Brad and Robbie found their prank very humorous. In fact, they were still laughing their heads off about it while hanging out together on the weekend. Then Brad had an idea for yet another practical joke.

"Why don't we put small dabs of glue on top of all the desks in homeroom class? The kids will spread out their pens and books, and when they try to put them away again at the end of the lesson, everything will be stuck to their desks!" Brad said.

"I'm not sure that's such a good plan either. It's not a good idea to mess around with glue—and we don't want a prank that damages other people's property or ends with a trip to the emergency room!" said Robbie.

Then Brad remembered that daylight saving time always began on the second Sunday in March, and he had an idea. He knew it was a winner!

"It was daylight saving last night," said Brad. "We turned all our clocks forward for summer. Let's tell the kids in our homeroom the wrong daylight saving time!"

"That sounds like a cool idea," said Robbie.

Brad and Robbie got to school early on Monday morning. They walked down the empty hallway and peered around the door of their homeroom to make sure nobody was inside.

Then Brad picked up a piece of chalk and wrote a notice on the blackboard that read: "Attention students! To fix a small but long-term inaccuracy in the way scientists have kept time around the world, the U.S. government decided that daylight savings would be different this year. All clocks would go forward two hours instead of the usual one hour. Unfortunately, the school caretaker forgot about this special change. So, when checking any school clock, please add an extra hour to find the correct time."

Afterward, Brad and Robbie had some time to kill before the teachers and the other kids arrived, so they went to library to study. However, they were so excited by their plan that they could barely concentrate at all. At last, the bell rang at 9:00 A.M.

When Brad and Robbie walked casually into their homeroom class, they found a spirited debate taking place.

"That's my seat," one girl was saying. "I always sit there during history class."

"Actually, it's my seat," said the boy standing on the other side of the chair. "It's ten o'clock, and I have math class now."

"No, it's nine o'clock," said the girl, pointing at the class clock. "This is my first class of the morning —history class."

"I guess you haven't heard either," said the boy, pointing to the notice on the blackboard. "Daylight savings was different this year. The classroom clock is wrong. It should say ten o'clock, not nine, and—"

"That's ridiculous," the girl interrupted.

The boy said, "Look, it's definitely ten o'clock, and I—"

Just then, Brad and Robbie's history teacher, Miss Fulton, entered the room. She sat down at her desk and took out her notes, then she said, "Good morning, class. Today we talk about the American Revolution."

Suddenly, the math teacher, Mr. Hogan, burst into the room, looking confused and apologizing profusely. When he saw Miss Fulton sitting at the desk, he looked even more puzzled than before. "One of my students came to fetch me. She said I was running an hour late for class! But now I see you are here, Miss Fulton, and the classroom clock says 9:00 A.M..."

Then Miss Fulton and Mr. Hogan noticed the message scrawled across the blackboard.

It wasn't long before everyone figured out that the kids had been the victims of a practical joke. There was no harm done, but the teachers weren't impressed. Brad and Robbie decided that it was probably best to put off playing any more pranks on their schoolmates for a while... well, at least until next term, anyway.

CHAPTER 3

One Last Prank?

The next day, Brad and Robbie had class in the computer room. When they arrived, all the other kids were already there. There was only one computer left and the two boys had to share it. They sat down at the machine and rummaged in their backpacks for their notes.

Soon, the class began, but after a while, Brad found that he had stopped listening to what the teacher was saying. He stared blankly at his computer screen and began to daydream about going the beach.

Suddenly, words began to appear on the screen in front of him. The message read: *"Is anyone there?"*

Brad's eyes grew wide with amazement. He nudged Robbie, who looked as if he was asleep, and pointed at the screen. Robbie's mouth fell open. Both boys looked around the room, but it seemed that nobody else had noticed anything unusual. No one was watching them, and all their classmates were focused on their own computer screens. Robbie peeked over the shoulder of the girl sitting next to him. She was making a boring flow chart about the production of paper. The message hadn't appeared on her screen.

Brad put his fingers on the keyboard and began to type. *"It's Brad and Robbie. Who are you?"* he wrote.

More words appeared on the screen. *"We are aliens from the planet of Zolton. We have come to study life on your planet."*

Brad and Robbie's eyes grew wider. They turned and stared at each other with their mouths open.

"I thought we agreed—no more practical jokes for a while," Brad hissed at Robbie.

"This has nothing to do with me, I promise," Robbie hissed back at him.

"What do you want?" Robbie typed back.

"We are very different from Earth people. We have three eyes, not two, and our skin is like that of the creatures you Earthlings call snakes. We have chosen you for a special mission. We plan to take you back to Zolton in our spaceship, so we can study you—"

Suddenly, Brad felt something slither over his shoulder—or so he thought. He nearly jumped out of his skin, but he was too scared to look behind. Then there was a small snigger from somewhere on the other side of the room. Brad peered over the top his computer screen at the girl sitting opposite him. She seemed strangely familiar. Then Brad remembered where he'd seen her before. It was the girl from the lunchroom who had found the worm in her apple! She looked up at him and winked.

"Uh-oh," said Robbie.

Brad glanced around at the perfectly normal human hand that had tapped him on the shoulder and looked up the arm to its owner's face.

Miss Fulton was standing behind them.

Standing beside Miss Fulton was the girl who had argued with the boy about the time. "Yesterday, you had some fun at our expense. Today, you are the entertainment," she said. "We switched the computer keyboards around. We plugged your keyboard into our computer, and our keyboard into your computer. We could see everything you typed, and vice versa. We are the aliens who have been sending you messages!"

"But how did you know we were responsible for the other pranks?" Brad and Robbie asked together.

"It wasn't hard," said one of the girls. "You were the only kids in class who didn't seem confused by the time switcheroo."

"Then we checked who was on lunch duty yesterday," the other girl said. "I bike to school with Robbie's sister, too. She told me all about the time he put blue food coloring in the milk to make her think it had gone all moldy and gross. You two are well known practical jokesters."

"Yesterday, you pulled pranks on us, but today, the joke's on you!" the two girls said together.

Miss Fulton appeared to be in on the joke, too. "Honestly, boys," she said, shaking her head and grinning, "You two scare much too easily. Don't you know there's no such thing as aliens?"

Soon, Brad and Robbie began to see the funny side, too. They had to admit that if they were going to play practical jokes on people, they had to accept that they would get pranks pulled on them as well.

"You know," said Brad, "I think the funniest jokes are the ones you don't see coming!"

Summarize

Use details from the story to summarize the important events in *The Joke's on You.* Your Point of View Chart may help you.

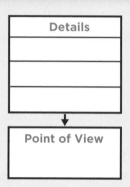

Details

↓

Point of View

Text Evidence

1. What kind of fiction is *The Joke's on You*? Which details tell you this? GENRE

2. What point of view do you think the author has toward practical jokes? Use details from the text to explain your answer. POINT OF VIEW

3. What does the idiom "time to kill" on page 8 mean? IDIOMS

4. At the end of the story, do you think Brad and Robbie are able to see things from a different perspective? Do they come to understand things from other people's point of view? If so, how? WRITE ABOUT READING

Compare Texts
Read a humorous poem about why a student claims she can't hand in her report on time.

The Homework Blues

I don't have a report to hand in,
I'm sorry to have to say.
It's not my fault at all,
I'm having a terrible day.

It all started this morning
when my alarm didn't go off.
So I carried on quietly sleeping
then woke with a terrible cough.

My coughing woke my dog
and he started chasing his tail,
which scared my baby sister
and she began to wail.

17

Mom ran to see the baby,
her eyes were wide with fear
She twisted her ankle badly,
which brought on a flood of tears.

With Baby and Mom both crying,
our family was in a state.
It took a while to settle down,
which made me run quite late.

I dashed out the door
with a piece of toast in my mouth.
As I ran down the sidewalk,
I saw my bus drive south.

I had no choice but to jog
the fifteen blocks to school.
I got all hot and sweaty,
and I felt like a giant fool!

When I was nearly here,
I dropped my bag on the ground.
Everything fell out
and scattered all around.

My report blew up in the air
and landed in a tree.
A bird picked it up in its beak
and flew far out to sea.

So now I have no report,
but I brought you an apple instead.
This day is a total disaster—
I just want to go back to bed!

Make Connections

What makes the events that the author tells about in *The Homework Blues* funny? ESSENTIAL QUESTION

Which was funnier, the story about practical jokes or the poem? Explain your answer. TEXT TO TEXT

Focus on Literary Elements

Rhyme Poetry is language that is arranged into patterns. Some poems rhyme. A poem that tells a story is called a narrative poem. Narrative poems often rhyme, because a rhyme pattern can give a poem a sense of moving forward.

Read and Find *The Homework Blues* is a narrative poem that is written in rhyme. Each group of four lines is called a stanza. In every stanza, the words at the end of the second and fourth lines rhyme. Find the rhyming words, and then read the poem aloud to hear the rhymes clearly.

Your Turn

Write your own narrative poem. Write about a day when everything went wrong. You can write about real people and events that really happened or you can make things up. Remember that a narrative poem tells a story. Try to make the words at the ends of some lines rhyme.